T0193221

The Millennial Christian Devotional Vol. 1

Belongs to _____

THE MILLENNIAL CHRISTIAN
Devotional

NINETY-DAY INTERACTIVE

Devotional FOR TODAY'S

CHRISTIAN MILLENNIAL

Brittany S. Dodson

VOL. 1

WESTBOW
PRESS®
A DIVISION OF THOMAS NELSON
& ZONDERVAN

WestBow Press books may be ordered through booksellers or by contacting:

WestBow Press
A Division of Thomas Nelson & Zondervan
1663 Liberty Drive
Bloomington, IN 47403
www.westbowpress.com
844-714-3454

Scripture quotations are taken from The Holy Bible, English Standard Version® (ESV®), Copyright © 2001 by Crossway, a publishing ministry of Good News Publishers. All rights reserved.

Author Photo Credit: Nelly Hernandez Photography

Cover Designer: Jason Marshall
Marshall Creative Group

ISBN: 978-1-6642-9672-5 (sc)
ISBN: 978-1-6642-9673-2 (hc)
ISBN: 978-1-6642-9674-9 (e)

Library of Congress Control Number: 2023906216

Print information available on the last page.

WestBow Press rev. date: 04/27/2023

Dedicated to

my family, a group of my biggest supporters,
confidants, and friends.
Thank you, and I love you.

Contents

A Message for Millennials   ix

Preface   xi

Four Benefits of this Devotional   xiii

Section 1   Let's Be Honest   1

Section 2   Going Deeper   21

Section 3   Staying Focused   55

Epilogue: Strength for the Journey   93

Five Tips for Studying God's Word   95

About the Author   97

A Message for Millennials

Is church *really* necessary? This question is asked amongst many millennials today. A number of millennials question the validity of church assemblies, the hearts of those who congregate in these assemblies, and the need to gather in the midst of others when God is present everywhere. Cultural shifts have allowed for the acceptance of a mass mind-set that deviates from "the norm" to embrace an overwhelming craving for individuality. Even if this comes at the cost of one of the beneficial precepts of the faith—going to church. And when this happens, we must be prepared to wrestle with these concerns, address them and their root appropriately, and provide an answer that is backed by scripture and reinforced by God's love. Knowing this begs a few questions: Is church assembly a mandate for the Christian believer? Why were churches established in the first place? And are they still necessary apart from being obligatory?

When we look at the New Testament church—visible and invisible—we can conclude that it is the core of God's program. In the church is where we see God's purposes and works come together, especially in Acts. In the local assembly, there's the opportunity to discover, grow in, and express spiritual gifts, which in turn, builds up the body of Christ (Acts 2:42, 46; 1 Corinthians 11—12, 14; Ephesians 4). Jesus Himself made a habit of going to church (Luke 4:16), and He should be the ultimate example for all professed believers.

As believers, we are to demonstrate a love and reverence for the Lord that shows our appreciation for Him. This should prompt us to want to get to know Him, and to do this, we must hear from those who have been called by Him to teach and help guide us. They would be the Pauls and Timothies, if you will, of our day called to instruct us on how to become Pauls and Timothies to perpetuate the fruitfulness of the gospel.

Although some have come to understand the value and importance of corporate worship, it would be derelict to dismiss the concern of those who question the need for corporate worship. Culture and even the church itself have played a part in feeding the mind-set of individualism causing some Christian millennials to turn away from experiencing God corporately with other believers to wanting to experience Him in the confines of their own homes. And while going to church doesn't assure salvation, it is one of the many proofs of salvation. A salvation that calls us to be readily on guard to gather with, exhort, encourage, intercede and watch for, and even correct our brothers and sisters.

So, amid hard truths and seeking resolves for the absence of millennials in church, what message can be sent to convey the importance of going to church? The only message that is the most effective and has proven to withstand the test of time is the message of the gospel of Jesus Christ. Although not viewed to be as efficacious as offering a coffee bar, Jesus is the best headliner for necessitating the critical nature of worshipping and learning of Him alongside other believers. He is the risen Savior that breathes life into our dead and sinful flesh and osmotically transforms our very nature into one that seeks daily to imitate Him. He is the one who hears what our soul cries and has an answer for each of our tears. He is God. He is the I Am. He is our rest on the Sabbath. He is all. And He is enough.

Preface

While I hold to the belief that there is not a different gospel for different eras, cultural shifts, or people groups, I do believe that how we contextualize the gospel affects how we witness about this gospel. It influences our evangelistic approach, shapes the efficacy of our witness, and harmoniously weaves together hearts eager to love and serve the Lord.

Over the next thirteen weeks, my prayer is that these devotionals help you to see yourself in view of who God is and who He needs you to be in today's times. As a millennial who is a Christ follower, I feel a sense of urgency and a sacrificial duty to spread the gospel in a relatable yet faithful way. Relatable through life experiences. But faithful to the scriptures. Faithful to the times. And faithful to God's people.

On the surface, this devotional may appear to be exclusively for millennials (because it literally says that!). But the goal of this devotional is to encourage all believers to keep fighting the good fight of faith with the Lord on their side. And the hope is also to reach and move those of any age to view God for who He has been, is, and will always be in light of the things they have experienced or are experiencing in life.

So, millennial or not, as you interact with this devotional, I invite you to journey along with me as we continue (or start) our journey with the Lord.

—Brittany D.

$\mathscr{Four}$ benefits
OF THIS DEVOTIONAL

1. It uses real world examples to convey a spiritual message.
   - Using Jesus's example of speaking in parables, this devotional seeks to do the same. It relates to you while relaying the message of the gospel.

2. It uses scripture to undergird the importance of seeing Christ in all that we do.
   - Who better to look to when navigating this world than the Creator of it? This devotional gives scriptural context to our life experiences to help us see God in everything around us.

3. It's interactive and allows for self-examination.
   - When seeking to grow, it always helps to pinpoint exactly where we want to grow from. By using prompts that cause us to look within, this devotional helps us to uncover who we are so that we can move toward being who God needs us to be.

4. It offers encouragement and hope for everyone.
   - This devotional is not just for believers. It seeks to reach even those who may be on the fence about getting to know Christ. Each week points us to Jesus—the Savior who died for all.

SECTION 1
LET'S BE HONEST

The Guilty Millennial   3

The Shame Millennial   9

The Redeemed Millennial   15

SECTION 2
GOING DEEPER

The Strong Millennial   23

The Competitive Millennial   29

The Successful Millennial   35

The Gifted Millennial   41

The Honorable Millennial   49

SECTION 3
STAYING FOCUSED

The Torn Millennial: Part 1   57

The Torn Millennial: Part 2   63

The Tempted Millennial: Part 1   71

The Tempted Millennial: Part 2   79

The Sexually Tempted Millennial   85

WEEKLY DEVOTIONS

Section

One

Let's Be Honest

The Guilty MILLENNIAL

DEVOTION

> Repentant tears wash out the stain of guilt.
> —Saint Augustine

I'm not sure if you watch a lot of television, but I'm somewhat of an addict; I love it like kids love toys! (Sounds like I may need to do some fasting, huh?) But as much as I hate to admit it, television has sewn its way into my heart, secured a tight stitch, and is now a permanent part of my life. One of my regular TV shows to watch is *Law & Order: SVU.* And a line that is used quite often in reference to a potential perpetrator, better known as "the perp," is "innocent until proven guilty."

Most of the time the first person questioned on the show is not the person who committed the crime. We begrudgingly sit through about three interviews, a foot chase or two, and seemingly never-ending commercials. And with each new person introduced, we unsuccessfully attempt to guess who the guilty party is until they are finally revealed. Even though, by then, those of us on the other side of the screen know who the suspect is, the jury still must find this person guilty. But unlike the fictional narrative of *Law & Order* that requires a person to be found guilty, the reality of our lives outside of Christ stands to show that we *are* guilty.

Our nature as humans causes us to conform to a way of thinking that says that our actions and the sins we commit are what make us unclean, impure, imperfect, and unholy. While it can be somewhat reassuring to believe that as long as we are good people who do good things, we will not be considered anything less than good, that is untrue. It is not the sinful acts that we commit that make us unclean and unholy in the face of a holy God. We come here unclean and imperfect, and that is what causes us to commit these sinful acts. We are born guilty until we are *born again.*

Guilty, per *Oxford's English Dictionary,* is defined as being justly chargeable with a particular fault or error. As the offspring of Adam, we acquire a death sentence that none of us come close to being able to satisfy, but Christ can and did. Romans 5:16 says: "And the free gift is not like the result of that one man's sin. For the judgment following one trespass brought condemnation, but the free gift following many trespasses brought justification." Just by being a descendant of Adam, we are guilty and worthy of condemnation. Scripture teaches us that we were condemned to death because of Adam's sin. And even though we haven't committed the same exact sin as Adam, we acquire death as judgment if we are not reconciled to God (Romans 5:14). Whether we like it or not, Adam's disobedience is what made us sinners, and because of this, we are born into the world spiritually dead. But Christ's one act of obedience provides us a way of escape from this. When we confess and accept Christ, we receive the free gift of salvation that brings justification. And justification is what makes us innocent and saves us from the guilt of sin. There's nothing that we can offer of ourselves, and there are not enough works that can be performed to achieve justification separate from Christ. To adopt this way of thinking would be to acquiesce to the mind-set of the Pharisees and declare ourselves righteous before God because of what *we* do instead of what Christ has done. But it's only being in right standing with God that makes us righteous, nothing else.

In all of our lives, we've done things that we are guilty of. First John 1:8 tells us that "if we say we have no sin, we deceive ourselves, and the truth is not in us." And then in verse 10, we're reminded of this again but in stronger terms. We're told that if we declare this, then we are calling God a liar, and His words cannot abide in us because He is truth. So, this just goes to show that we are all guilty of something, and even if we say we aren't, we are made guilty by that assertion alone. This should void us of any ego or the refusal to go to God for forgiveness to be reconciled to Him. But even though we are guilty of things that have separated us from God, we don't have to continue to live this way. We don't have to allow our guilt to determine the trajectory of our lives. Christ's death intercepted the punishment of condemnation and freed us from all guilt and shame. And His life is what allows us to live in the fullness of this freedom. That is something we should embrace with gladness and thankfulness each and every day.

Although *Law & Order* is an enjoyable crime drama and, for the most part, they seem to get it right when it comes to vindicating the innocent and punishing the guilty, I believe it's reassuring to know that the fate of our souls is not in the hands of a human judge. The confidence we can have that Christ has done the satisfactory work on the cross to clear us of all sin and guilt brings hope. And the comfort in knowing that God is the supreme, just judge who declares us not guilty brings joy to any believer's heart.

DOING THE WORK: GUILT

PRAYER

Dear Lord,

Thank You for sending Your Son, Jesus Christ, to release me from the guilt of my sins. I want to live each day with an appreciation for the sacrifice that was made on my behalf. I want to live life boldly and freely because I have been justified and made righteous by You. Help me to fully embrace this as I continue to embrace You and all that You have done. And as I do this, help others to know that through You, they can be found not guilty, too.

THINGS TO CONSIDER:

1. Am I dealing with feeling guilty because of things in my past?
2. Does my view of salvation and justification mirror that of the Pharisees at all?
3. Is there anything in my life that I am guilty of that I have not sincerely confessed to God?

SCRIPTURES TO READ:

- Isaiah 53:5
- Romans 5
- 1 John 1:8–10

My Notes

My Notes

DEVOTION

> Instead of your shame there shall be a double portion; instead of dishonor they shall rejoice in their lot; therefore in their land they shall possess a double portion; they shall have everlasting joy.
>
> —Isaiah 61:7 ESV

September is always a highly anticipated month each year. It marks the beginning of fall and all the readily enjoyable festivities that follow its entrance. For those who aren't too fond of the heat, the insects, or the sweaty, smelly clothing that sticks to your skin, this month brings joy to your heart. If you haven't figured it out by now, I am one of those people. Each breath of cool, crisp, dry fall air brings a pleasantry that summer just fails to produce. Alongside the pleasantry of the fall air are the memories that begin to surface as each wave of a slight breeze lightly sweeps across the visible parts of my body, and I am caught in the middle of trying to decide whether I need to wear a jacket or keep rocking the short-sleeved T-shirt with sandals.

With each breeze, the memories that suddenly flood my brain are of my college years. I'm taken back to that beautiful UCA campus. The nicely manicured grounds. The students— some seriously entrenched in their studies, others just ready for the next party. The meticulously sculpted buildings housing the classrooms that served as the catalysts for solidifying our goals and dreams. The dormitories that infinitesimally represented our home away from home. I'm reminded of the friends, experiences, good times, and laughs that college afforded me and how those friends, experiences, good times, and laughs helped to shape who I am today. But when the floodgates open, and all the good memories come rushing in, they don't come alone. With them come those memories that slowly cause a shift in my composure, a delay in my reaction, and a moment of that daunting, thrashing, exhausting emotion: shame.

If I'm being honest, I would have to say that college brought about some of the best times of my life. But some of my most shameful moments were also birthed during that time. I once would pride myself on being the "I would never" person until I was the "I wish I wouldn't have" person. I dove into waters that exposed my inability to swim. And I opened myself to painful lacerations that would become deeper wounds that only the blood of Jesus could heal.

When we dig into how we should approach shame, we are able to uncover, to the best of our descriptive ability, the true definition of the love Christ showed on Calvary. Although we're unable to fully comprehend, it's easy to accept that only an infinite God could love an intentionally sinful, inappreciative, imperfect wreck to the point of sending His Son just to get that wreck back into right standing with Him. Shame causes us to feel dishonorable, disgraceful, and just dirty. And if we're honest with ourselves, this shame doesn't come unjustifiably. It comes because of our sin. Sin causes shame. It feeds shame. And, in a space devoid of Christ, it validates it. It makes you want to hide and run away in isolation. There's a towering hesitation to share this space with anyone because just as our shame cries out to be heard, the silence of our humiliation is louder. Shame is overwhelming, but thank God that Christ is overcoming.

When we read Romans 8:1, it inspires a new feeling that eclipses our shame—hope. Hope for all of us who understand that shame is a form of self-condemnation that Christ has put to death once and for all. It tells us that "there is therefore now no condemnation for those who are in Christ Jesus" (Romans 8:1).

We must come to terms with our lives as sinners who have been set free. Actively participating in sin should cause shame simply because that is not God's intended design for our lives as His creation. We feel shame because the inward part of us that senses and is consciously aware of God knows that sin isn't right or good for us. But once we accept Christ as our Savior, we are brought back into a covenant relationship with God allowing His Spirit to reign in us and rule over us. And with His Spirit comes the removal of the reign of shame. This is the same Spirit that Romans 8:2 says "sets us free" because we are now in Christ and no longer in sin.

Recognizing that our shame is a feeling that can cause us to undervalue the sacrifice of Christ helps us to truly embrace the sacrifice of Christ. Of course, it would be negligent for anyone to think that our old lives could no longer cause us to lament over the things that took us away from what we knew was right. But that lamentation should neither consume nor direct our heart posture toward God or override the magnitude of our salvation experience.

Because we are made new, our shame that rode in along with our sin was nailed to the cross with the Savior who carried our sin and shame for us. He knew we would feel this way. He knew we would experience moments of dejection and repugnance. But He also knew that His grace would clothe us. His love would comfort us. And His Spirit would keep us. Shame does not have a place in Christ, and it should no longer have a hold on you. So, embrace those memories that bring on those subtle smiles and quiet laughs while thanking God for forgetting those that don't.

DOING THE WORK: SHAME

PRAYER

Dear Lord,

Help me to live in the now of my salvation and the glory of Your sacrifice. I understand that my sin has caused me to feel shame, but I know that in You I have been forgiven and set free. Help me to embrace this freedom with joy, live in it with confidence, and share it with love. I know that Your Word says that whom the Son sets free is free indeed. So today, I give my shame to You so that I can enjoy the abundance of honor that comes with serving You.

THINGS TO CONSIDER:

1. Am I dealing with shame because of things in my past or because of how I feel about myself?
2. Have I forgiven myself for past sins and given that over to God to heal?
3. What steps can I take to move forward in Christ and live freely while acknowledging the root of my shame?

SCRIPTURES TO READ:

- Psalm 34:4–5
- Isaiah 50:7
- Isaiah 61:7
- Romans 8:1
- Romans 10:11

My Notes

My Notes

Week 3

DEVOTION

> For even the Son of Man came not to be served
> but to serve, and to give His life as a ransom for
> many.
>
> —Mark 10:45 ESV

If you've watched any of the *Taken* movies or any crime drama series, you've probably seen your fair share of someone taking something from someone else to leverage them to pay some sort of ransom. The kidnapper/thief picks up the phone, disguises their voice, and demands a substantial amount of money in exchange for whatever was taken. Some deem whatever was taken valuable enough to pay the ransom as soon as demanded; others call in law enforcement and hold out to weigh their options, and some just flat-out refuse. But in any case, these time-sensitive situations require some sort of action.

When we think about ransoms, what normally happens is that an innocent person or a precious inanimate object is seized to strike fear or desperation into the heart of someone else. The person being asked to pay the ransom will do all that he or she can for this innocent person or object to be released and brought back to safety (because it's assumed that nothing has been done to warrant the kidnapping/theft in the first place). But what's so awesome about the ransom that Jesus paid on behalf of the sins of the world is that every man, woman, boy, and girl in the world is not innocent, but Jesus still paid the price to have us freed from the captivity of sin and the wrath of God.

One beautiful story of redemption that also foreshadows the universal reign of Christ through David is the story of Ruth and Boaz. Two central themes in the book of Ruth are those of kindness and redemption. If you recall, Ruth was a Moabite woman who was married to one of Naomi's two sons. Naomi's husband and sons all died leaving her widowed with two daughters-in-law, one of which (Orpah) wanted to return home to her people. But Ruth stayed. Clothed in the words "where you go I will go, and where you lodge I will lodge," are the love and loyalty Ruth showed toward her mother-in-law. By Ruth showing this loyalty and kindness to Naomi, she put herself in a position to be shown kindness by Boaz, Naomi's deceased husband's relative. Boaz welcomed Ruth and acted as a kinsman-redeemer for her. So what was once a desperate situation for Naomi and Ruth now turned into favor and fullness. Ruth and Boaz would father Obed who would become heir to the property of Naomi's husband and also the grandfather of King David. And this king gets us to our King who is our kinsman-redeemer.

If you were to compare Naomi and Ruth's situation to that of ours and those who have had something taken from them, a common theme, among many others, arises—desperation. If we're honest, our lives in the absence of accepting the redemptive work of Christ on the cross reflects that of bitterness, emptiness, restlessness, and tumult. Before salvation, we were desperate for answers, peace, joy, and satisfaction that we just couldn't seem to find in the things of the world. And anyone who still hasn't accepted this work is still searching for these things. But this is exactly why Christ died, because He knew this. He knew that a life held captive by sin would only result in death—spiritual, emotional, financial, physical, relational, mental. All areas. Nothing good can result from sinfulness, and until we truly accept this, we will continue to seek what we will never find in other people, places, and things. The redemptive work of Christ saves us from desperation and brings us into a place of tranquility. When we choose Christ, we no longer have to chase a hope that says we'll find what we're missing because Christ is the hope that we've been missing all along. He is literally all that we need.

If you're a believer now, you can think back on your "BC" (before Christ) days and say with confidence that you were in desperate need of rescuing. You needed someone to come and pay the ransom for you to be set free. And thanks be to God that He sent His Son, in the flesh, as our kinsman-redeemer, to do just that. Christ came at the appointed time, as God and man, to pay the price for His people to be released from the master of sin. First Peter 1:18–19 reminds us of this: "knowing that you were ransomed from the futile ways inherited from your forefathers, not with perishable things such as gold and silver, but with the precious blood of Christ like that of a lamb without blemish or spot." Unlike those who are taken and the ransom paid with corruptible items, Christ paid our ransom with His incorruptible life through the shedding of His blood. As a rightful King, He humbled Himself to the point of death to buy our freedom. He gave His life so that we could have life more abundantly. He got up so that we can live again. All of which is a debt that we can never repay and are not expected to repay. He just wants our life, which was given by Him, to be given in service to Him.

I know that most of us love a good story with a happy ending. But despite how gratifying the movies and the TV shows are, whenever we witness a victim safely retrieve all that has been taken from him or her, the story of redemption for the believer is far better. And not just because the sacrifice was greater but because it's everlasting and eternal.

DOING THE
WORK: REDEEMED

PRAYER

Dear Lord,

I just want to stop and thank You for the sacrifice of Your Son, Jesus Christ. I don't know where I would be had it not been for Your saving grace. I know that I don't always seem to be appreciative, but I acknowledge today that my life would not be the same without You. Thank You, Jesus, for paying the price for me. And even though I can never repay You, I will work to give my life in service to You each day.

THINGS TO CONSIDER:

1. Do I live each day with an appreciation for the sacrifice of Christ and what it does for me?
2. Have I grown to fully understand the magnitude of the sacrifice of Jesus Christ?
3. Could I do more to witness to others about the redemptive work of Christ?

SCRIPTURES TO READ:

- The book of Ruth
- 1 Peter 1:17–21

My Notes

My Notes

Section

Going Deeper

Week 4

DEVOTION

> No man is an island, Entire of itself, Every man is
> a piece of the continent, A part of the main.
> —John Donne

In today's time, it is good to be reminded of the existence of a higher power: God. And we should also be reminded of an important aspect of humanity: community. The beginning of this poem by John Donne conveys to us the vital role we, as human beings, play in one another's lives. And it also emphasizes how we are only as strong as our acceptance of the benefit that comes by leaning on others for help. Because we are so hard-pressed to be productive, useful, valued, seen, and heard, we tend to think that we must do things on our own to come by these results. We are told to be strong, and we've been deceived into thinking that strength means going it alone. But these things couldn't be further from the truth.

In Paul's second letter to the church at Corinth, he dispels the idea of being puffed up in our own strength. Paul tells of a vision he had, and he made sure that as he shared this, he let his audience know that in his boasting, he was only boasting of his weaknesses. Today, we seem to think that making mention of ourselves to others or highlighting our best moments on Facebook and Instagram are the marks of strength. But if we take notes from Paul, who was taught by one of the premier teachers of the Law, Gamaliel, we will realize that all our accolades and strengths outside of Christ, in Paul's words, are "counted but dung." So, they literally mean nothing.

There are so many reasons we tend to want to display our strengths and hide our weaknesses. One reason is that we live to live up to the expectations of others. This is one that I have had to strive daily to cast down. The thought that I couldn't be anything but strong and perfect before others began to be a burden that I could no longer carry. And it's the opposite of how God wants us to come to Him. God wants us to realize how weak and poor in spirit we are so that He can be the one to fill us and give us strength. In laboring to be who others expect us to be, we are discounting that they are just like us and in need of someone stronger and mightier than themselves.

Another reason some feel the need to always display strength is because of the dependency others have on them. Some people tend to be the backbone of their families, communities, churches, and other spaces they operate in. If this is you, this capacity calls for you to be strong and to be strong *a lot*! You don't have the luxury of taking a day off or showing signs of weakness because just as you begin to slip into a moment of weakness, you must quickly gather yourself so that you can be there for someone else. But you must realize that even though you are doing this for others, this is not God's way; neither is it healthy for any one person to always be the strength for others. That's not your all-encompassing role; it's God's. And just like others need someone to lean on, so do you.

As Paul addresses the congregants at Corinth in his letter, he is not only speaking of weaknesses, but he also brings out what undergirds our admission of weakness: humility. As Paul is outlining his vision, he says that to keep him from becoming conceited, he is given a "thorn in the flesh." Although scholars are unsure of exactly what this "thorn" is, Paul made sure we knew why it was given to him: to keep him humble. And then he goes on to tell us that he pleaded with God three times to take it away, but God's response to him was one that only a God of all knowledge and power could give. He said to Paul, "My grace is sufficient for you, for My power is made perfect in weakness." God knows that He is always present in the life of the believer and that His grace will never run out, so He can say in confidence that no matter how critical the circumstance, He will always be there as our strength. And He says this with absolute certainty and assurance. Paul was confident that as a mere human, in his weakest hour, God would avail Himself as the almighty, supreme God He is. And Paul also knew that our earthly strength can't come close to matching the most miniscule display of God's power. This is how Paul knew that he could trust the words of his heavenly Father.

I know it seems as though being strong in our own might is how we portray to others the image of greatness, but this doesn't fall in line with the character of Christ or with our duty as believers. Just as we garner strength from fully relying on the Lord, we also are told to rely on one another. Galatians 6:2 calls us to bear one another's burdens, which means we will all have them at some point. Ephesians 6:18 tells us to watch for and supplicate for all saints. We are commissioned to use our weapons of prayer and discernment on behalf of other believers. In this, we are all interceding for another as a way of strengthening the body of Christ. And if we need more motivation to become weak, we can look no further than our Suffering Servant. Christ Himself showed the power of weakness by suffering so that we could share in abundant comfort (2 Corinthians 1:5). His sacrifice reminds us that as humans, we don't have to be strong for anyone else, we just need to acknowledge our weaknesses before Him. True strength comes in our weakest moments because this is when we honestly acknowledge that Christ always and consistently exists as our strength.

DOING THE
WORK: STRONG

PRAYER

Dear Lord,

Help me to dismiss the idea that I must rely on my own strength to do all things. I want to start today acknowledging that You are all powerful. I know that You said in Your Word that You are my strength. So, Father, forgive me for working so hard to exalt myself above Your sovereignty and strength. As I continue on this journey with You, I want to yield all that I am to You and fully give myself to You for You to be my strength each day and always.

THINGS TO CONSIDER:

1. Are there areas in my life that I need to give over to God to be my strength?
2. Do I need to work on being more humble in my life?
3. Does my community, family, friends, or church family play a part in me always feeling the need to be strong?

SCRIPTURES TO READ:

- 2 Corinthians 1:3–7
- 2 Corinthians 12
- Ephesians 6:10, 18

My Notes

My Notes

Week 5

DEVOTION

> Don't strive to be superior to others; strive to be better than you were yesterday.
> —Matshona Dhliwayo

If we're honest, we all know someone who has a competitive spirit or lives for comparison. That person who reluctantly or never compliments others because he or she secretly wishes to have seen *insert whatever item you choose* before anyone else. The neighbor who sees what someone else in the neighborhood does, steals the idea, and then tries to 1-up the original version of what he or she saw. Or those who always cast aspersions on others to feel better about themselves. At any rate, we've more than likely experienced this at some point in our lives or we've been this person at one point in time (if not still). What I didn't realize was that Paul addressed this attitude in his second letter to the Corinthian church. And while I had previously read both letters to the church at Corinth multiple times, this time Paul's words stood out in a way that they hadn't before. When studying God's Word, the purpose behind a revelation doesn't always come when the revelation itself comes, but nonetheless, when the time comes to unveil it to others, God shows you exactly why He made it known to you in the first place. (I realize now that it was because I was going to be writing this devotional).

In 2 Corinthians 10:12–13, Paul says this: "Not that we dare to classify or compare ourselves with some of those who are commending themselves. But when they measure themselves by one another and compare themselves with one another, they are without understanding. But we will not boast beyond limits, but will boast only with regard to the area of influence God assigned to us, to reach even to you." Here, Paul completely invalidated the idea of unhealthy comparison and competition. His sentiment toward this trivial mind-set is coined by the words "they are without understanding." But how?

In this passage, the Greek word for "to compare," is *sugkrinó*, which is derived from "sýn" or "identified with" and "krínō" or "to judge." We can conclude that comparing here is discriminately judging one thing in connection to another. A part of how we are without understanding when we compare ourselves to others is due to the lack of absolute knowledge we have of all things. To compare ourselves to others or compete with others would be to do this from our own perspective, bias, and opinion, all of which are limited by our finite makeup. Making an unjust or prejudiced comparison lacks wisdom and truth, hence why Paul would speak so strongly against it. To compete with others, we would do this based upon a comparison that is formed upon the idea that what someone else is doing is not as good as how we can or will do it. And we do this based upon how we see ourselves, which is not always discerned from an honest view.

When we look at verse 13 of this passage, Paul makes a point to show us that God has given particular assignments. And to those people within the scope of those assignments, they were not going to boast about anything beyond what God had given them directly for them to share. They didn't look at the excellence, or lack thereof, of others as their barometer of success. They kept their eyes and their measurable standard locked onto someone they knew they should imitate and long to be like—Christ. If you really think about what verse 13 says, it's almost as if Matshona was just echoing the words of Paul. Paul and the apostles were only striving daily to be better than who they were the day before. I can only venture to say that they worked hourly to be more like Christ because their mission was enveloped in this one goal. After all, the Bible teaches us that we are being transformed from one degree of glory to another (2 Corinthians 3:18). So, we are to strive to become more like Christ until the final unveiling of our immortality when Christ returns for

His people. And this is exactly what Paul was trying to convey—that those who claim Christ should work to become more like Christ, not better than their fellow brother or sister.

Let's be honest, folks. Today, social media is the breeding ground for competition and comparison. It causes us to take a deep dive into our own lives to see if we're doing things the right way and for enough people. We begin to obsessively ask ourselves how we can do something greater, fresher, or newer than the next person. That's why it may be a wise decision from time to time to step away from it all to restore within us God's view for the course of our lives. I know it can be a shortcoming of our flesh to want to outshine, outdo, or compare ourselves to those around us, but this is a condition of the heart that must be addressed and redirected. When we get caught up in competition and comparison, we are (1) making ourselves the standard instead of Christ, (2) not leaving ourselves much room for growth by always making others, who are just like us, our measuring stick, and (3) disproportionately forming an opinion about ourselves while devaluing other image bearers. It takes a level of boldness to do this that Paul and the other apostles didn't have and didn't need. They were confident in boasting in the Lord and working toward a greater end because they knew whose approval was ultimately needed. Paul proves this by saying, "For it is not the one who commends himself who is approved, but the one whom the Lord commends."

DOING THE
WORK: COMPETITIVE

PRAYER

Dear Lord,

I ask that you help me to identify and cast down the need to compare myself to others. If I am dealing with the spirit of competitiveness, help me to be reassured in You that how You have made me is enough. I pray that I can walk in confidence in what You have called me to do and who You have called me to be. I want to embrace Your purpose for my life so that I can help other image bearers live from Your calling on their lives and not from what they see others do.

THINGS TO CONSIDER:

1. Do I struggle with comparing myself to others or competing with others?
2. What are some areas in my life that I feel inadequate in that cause me to compare myself to others?
3. How can identifying my purpose in the kingdom help me to not compare myself with and compete with others?

SCRIPTURES TO READ:

- Psalm 139:14
- 2 Corinthians 10
- Ephesians 2:10

My Notes

My Notes

The Successful MILLENNIAL

Week 6

DEVOTION

> For what does it profit a man to gain the whole
> world and forfeit his soul?
> —Mark 8:36 ESV

I have an exceptionally smart niece. Her observation and awareness of things and people around her and her ability to put these things into the proper situational context is remarkable. And although I have a reason to be biased, I am a relatively objective person so I'm not just saying this because she's related to me. I'm saying this because God has gifted her with something, and I can't wait to see how it manifests itself for the kingdom in the future. It reminds me of Psalm 8:2: "Out of the mouth of babies and infants, you have established strength." This line of this hymn highlights how God ordains the weakest instruments and vessels to reveal His glory. There is something about innocence that embodies true worship. And maybe by using those who are weakest, God knows that the message will be more readily received because it would only be by the power of God that a small child could speak words of wisdom and authority. And as words of wisdom go, my niece shared some with me not too long ago. She invited me to tag along on one of her weekend adventures, and I had to decline because of an engagement that I had to attend as the soloist. After the declination, her words to me were, "MeMe (that's what she calls me; don't ask why), you need to stop scheduling so much stuff and being so busy. You need to rest because if you keep having things to do, you'll just be more tired all the time." I guess I needed a six-year-old to tell me to take a break! But breaks are what those of us who are goal-oriented see as impediments to success.

A mind-set that has become increasingly popular amongst millennials is one that tells us that we must be busy to be successful. We do a lot! And although this can equate to us having a lot to offer, if we're honest, we are also more stressed and are experiencing a lot of burnout. Not too long ago, I was home sitting in bed, and the Spirit convicted me of taking on too many things. The Lord spoke to me and put in my heart the distinction between doing what I want to do versus doing what I'm supposed to do. In that moment, I was prompted to examine if these two things—what I want to do and what I'm purposed to do—were aligned. And when the Spirit of the Lord revealed this to me, I wanted to be sure I was obedient. But because I had already decided on these arbitrary deadlines in my mind for all of the things I wanted to do, I got a little sidetracked and was trying to slip back into grind mode. So, God sent a small messenger to remind me of what I needed to refocus my attention toward—His purpose for my life.

Let's look at an example of how our self-directed missions and measures of success don't always equate to that of God's. When Saul was king, Samuel went to him and told him that the Lord was instructing him to destroy the Amalekites. Saul was to spare no one and nothing. But Saul spared the king, Agag, and the best of the sheep, the calves, the lambs, and oxen instead of being obedient to God. To justify his actions, he told Samuel that they kept the best of the sheep and oxen to sacrifice to the Lord. This is a prime example to us of how disobedience to what God wants us to do, even if we think it's right, good, or will yield advantageous results, is wrong. And it also shows us how God doesn't approve what He doesn't give. Even as we work toward success, if God doesn't give the mission for us to accomplish, He isn't going to accept or bless it. So, what Saul saw as success, God rejected as rebellion. And Samuel made sure he pointed this out to him by telling him: "Has the Lord as great delight in burnt offerings and sacrifices, as in obeying the voice of the Lord? Behold, to obey is better than sacrifice, and to listen than the fat of rams. For rebellion is as the sin of divination, and presumption is as iniquity and idolatry. Because you have rejected the word of the Lord, He has also rejected you from being king."

There are two things that I've learned in working toward success. One is that success can sometimes be deception. We must be aware that open doors don't always come by God and greater opportunities aren't always afforded to us for us to do the Lord's work. Sometimes, it's the work of the enemy to keep us right where he wants us in our lives so that we don't completely surrender ourselves to the Lord. He wants us to stay broken, wounded, and sinful and will use success to manipulate us into thinking that our lives are on track with where God wants us to go. Remember that all that glitters is not gold and all that looks good is not God. This is why it's imperative that we get and keep ourselves in a place where we know that God is pleased with our lives and not just our works.

Another important lesson I learned after years of being inundated with this feeling is that constantly working toward success outside of God's direction stifles your ability to be able to celebrate grand moments because there's a part of you that still feels like it's not enough. Success for the person walking according to God's purpose always feels like success. But for the person feeling the pressure of success from a lack of self-confidence, external pressure, or an over-compensatory obligation, your mind translates success as failure. And that's because the drive to succeed wasn't inspired by God.

It's a task to grow to understand that what can't fill us can't satisfy within us the pride and sense of purpose that we seek. But if we will just seek to please God and succeed in doing the Lord's work, we will always be in a place of gratitude and contentment. On our journey to success, only one thing is necessary—closeness and fellowship with the Lord. This is what gives us our good portion—good portion of wisdom, knowledge, ideas, dreams, desires, plans, and success. This is what helps us to overcome the need to always be successful in man's eyes so that what we do will always be pleasing in God's.

DOING THE
WORK: SUCCESSFUL

PRAYER

Dear Lord,

I know that society says that I should do all that I can to be successful and stay ahead in the world. And I know that sometimes this attitude can filter over into the church. But God, I want to be all that I can be in the kingdom. I want to live from Your purpose and calling on my life. I don't want to succumb to the idea that I must gain things and praise to be satisfied. All I need is You and Your love. Draw me closer to the peace that I need to stay satisfied in You and You alone.

THING TO CONSIDER:

1. Have I fallen victim to the idea that I must be successful to be happy?
2. Do I work harder than I should because I am trying to accomplish things God isn't leading me to?
3. Has the idea and acquisition of success blinded me to areas in my life that I need to surrender to the Lord?

SCRIPTURES TO READ:

- Proverbs 16:3
- Matthew 6:33
- Mark 4:18–19

My Notes

My Notes

DEVOTION

> A man's gift makes room for him and brings him before the great.
> —Proverbs 18:16 ESV

Spiritual gifts are immensely powerful, beneficial, necessary weapons in the kingdom. They are unique supernatural workings of the Holy Spirit that allow the believer to demonstrate the power and glory of God. Our spiritual gifts are not only given by the Spirit and the Spirit alone, but there is a purpose and an aim for our gifts. It's not for us to be praised and known by people but for something to happen inwardly—within us, within those around us, and within the body of Christ. And in 1 Corinthians 12 and Ephesians 4, we see the goals of these gifts. They:

- equip the saints for the work of ministry,
- build up the body of Christ,
- unify us in the faith and the knowledge of the Son of God,
- grow us so that we aren't deceived and carried away from our true doctrine and,
- work in favor of the common good.

All these things should happen because of us properly using our gifts given by God. But there is a requirement of those who operate with a certain level of giftedness. This requirement often comes with the acknowledgment that sacrifice, obedience and discipline, intermittent isolation, boldness, and humility are all a part of walking in the divine calling that our gifts entail. And we'll take a moment to dig into each of these.

SACRIFICE

Whenever we step into a place where we are ready to truly give ourselves to the work of the Holy Spirit, we must understand that there are some things that we will have to give up. There is a cost. Following Christ and becoming an operative for the kingdom by using what God has gifted us with may mean we lose relationships, dreams, material possessions, or even our lives. In Luke 14, Jesus told those in the crowd to first consider what it would cost to be His disciple. He forewarned them that if they could not renounce certain things and persevere in faith that they could not be His disciple. Jesus is showing us that what God calls us to do is far greater than what we want to do or even what man may ask us to do. This takes complete commitment and total trust.

OBEDIENCE AND DISCIPLINE

In accepting and using our gifts, we must recognize that we must be disciplined and obedient to the teachings of Christ and the wisdom, guidance, and voice of the Holy Spirit always. Because after all, the Spirit is the one who empowers us with and allows us to utilize our gifts. So, it would just make sense to let Him be in control of the vessel that houses these gifts. Truly experiencing the joy of our gifts is directly proportionate to the discipline we have to operate in those gifts. We can't be negligent and disobedient to the call of God and expect to thrive in the joy of our calling. We must stay active in obedience and open to discipline, always.

INTERMITTENT ISOLATION

I'm sure you recall Jesus choosing moments of solitude over being with people. In preparation for the beginning of His ministry and before He was tempted by Satan, He spent forty days in the wilderness fasting (Luke 4:1–2). And before making an important decision and just to spend time alone to pray (Luke 6:12–13, Luke 5:16), Jesus withdrew Himself from others. So, if Jesus did it, then we must know that it's necessary for us to do as well, especially if we are gifted by God to perform certain tasks.

BOLDNESS

As gifted members of the body of Christ, a certain level of boldness must be present to carry out certain assignments. At times, it may seem a little uncomfortable and out of the norm to say or do certain things that the Spirit is leading you to do, but it wouldn't be supernatural if you felt empowered and comfortable in your own ability to do it. Your gift may require you to step outside of your own comfort zone or what's accepted by others, and fear may set in, but you must believe that through Christ, you can do all things that He has called you to do. Walking in boldness in your giftedness may also cause you to have to "do it afraid" because of the doubt that looms over you from others. There may come a time when those around you won't accept your gift(s) because of proximity and familiarity. But do not let them hinder you. Do not bury your gift. Do not let them awaken fear in you. And do not let people minimize your purpose because of their egos, insecurities, or reluctance to accept your calling.

HUMILITY

As we grow in areas of spiritual giftedness, we must be careful not to get puffed up within ourselves and see ourselves as the generator of our gifts. Thinking like this sometimes causes us to see Jesus as a product to be sold or branded instead of a Person to be accepted. And we tend to "put ourselves out there" instead of magnifying Christ. The Bible says that our gifts will make room for us and put us before great men. This means that when we begin to unselfishly operate in our giftedness and are obedient to the Holy Spirit, opportunities will present themselves for us to perpetually promote Christ, not ourselves. People will see the value in who we have to offer, will have an earnest hunger for what we share, and will want to provide us with the means and platform to keep sharing it.

The evincing of our gifts is wrapped in what Paul describes as "a more excellent way." As we journey from 1 Corinthians 12 to 13, we see that we should be functioning in love as it deals with our gifts. If what we're doing lacks love, it means nothing and is not helpful, and we want to be helpful. If we're going to accept our spiritual gifts, then we need to have the character and the love to support it. No excuses, no exceptions, or anything that justifies us not aligning with God's will and plan for His church and His people. We must remember that the function of our gifts God's way is more important than anything or anyone else. We don't want to be disorderly, proud, glory-seeking, or even unaware of the need as it deals with gifts in the body of Christ. We want to be impactful so that God's name is always praised, those in the body are uplifted and encouraged, and others outside of the body come to know Christ.

At first glance, it seems as though being gifted comes with a lot, but God has more than equipped you for the task because He has given you Himself to fill and empower you. No matter what anyone says or thinks, you must know that your assignment and operating in your gift is greater than anyone's acceptance. And this means yours, too. So, even if it doesn't make sense to you or anyone else right now, use your gift anyway. If it costs you a good time, use it anyway. If it feels hard to choose between the world, your flesh, and the gift that God has given you, choose your gift. Because when you operate in your realm of giftedness, you have the opportunity to reach so many people. By being obedient, we eliminate excuses, we cast out fear, we offer hope, and we continue to walk in the manner worthy of our gifts and calling.

DOING THE WORK: GIFTED

PRAYER

Dear Lord,

I just want to thank You for allowing me, an unworthy vessel, to carry the gift(s) You have given me. I pray for a heart that is always surrendered to You and is sensitive to Your voice and Your commands. Anoint me, use me, and consecrate me fully for Your service. God, create in me a heart that desires to always use my gifts so that I can bring others to know Your immense love and overflowing abundance of grace.

THINGS TO CONSIDER:

1. Do I feel that I am operating in my giftedness the way the Lord needs me to be?
2. What, if anything, is hindering me from fully accepting my gifts and calling?
3. Are there people in my life that are causing me to be afraid to walk in the authority of my gifts?

SCRIPTURES TO READ:

- 1 Corinthians 12
- Ephesians 4:1–16

My Notes

My Notes

Week 8

DEVOTION

> Finally, brothers, whatever is true, whatever is honorable, whatever is just, whatever is pure, whatever is lovely, whatever is commendable, if there is any excellence, if there is anything worthy of praise, think about these things.
> —Philippians 4:8 ESV

Paul was one of the most revered apostles of his time. And I can only imagine that as he was concluding his letter to the Philippian church from a Roman jail cell, the words of exhortation and thanksgiving filled his heart with pride and joy. It doesn't seem to make sense for Paul to be in good spirits from a jail cell, but his life's mission, after his conversion, was to bring as many people to Christ as possible even if that meant facing death. And to Paul, this was honorable.

In this letter to the church at Philippi, we see a lot of important prompts. But one that stands out is the call to be honorable that Paul issues in 4:8. When we think about being honorable in view of this verse, we must understand that Paul knew that his audience would be faced with a choice—a choice to think on things that are to be venerated or thinking on those that are not. And depending on which consumes our thoughts, one will inevitably determine what we do because it will mean that's what we value.

This draws my attention to how we use social media. While social media is amazing because of the amount of information we can share, it can be dangerous for this very reason. People all over the world have access to one another via electronic devices.

We share fashion hacks, home organization tips, Bible verses, trendy dances, and so many other valuable things that enhance all our lives. But then there are those things that may not be so helpful, not so honorable. No matter what form of social media you use—Facebook, Instagram, TikTok, etc.—you likely know the temptation to repost that funny meme that may contain content that's inappropriate for the Christian. Or that motivational post with a few expletives that may not agree with those graceful words we preach that the Christian ought to use. Or that not yet fact-checked post bashing a political candidate that we are not very fond of at the moment. Or maybe it's a statement full of truth but also full of offense that may hurt someone if shared too soon or at all. Regardless of the setting or content, as believers, we must practice self-control and use discretion, wisdom, discernment, and love in all that we say and do. We must be honorable.

Maybe you've mastered the art of thinking honorably, thereby living honorably. If so, you are living from the character of Christ, which is to be commended. But maybe this is a struggle for you, and you need a little encouragement to walk in dignity on a daily basis. Don't feel bad; you aren't alone. Many Christians contend with allowing corrupt, deceptive, dishonest thoughts to slip through their spiritual cracks without reinforcing rebuke. As we allow this to continue to take place, the more dishonor will manifest itself in our lives. This is why Paul urges his audience to think on these pleasing things because he knew that there would come a time when the opportunity presented itself for them not to. Trust me, I understand that we may not set out to intentionally think or act dishonorably. We may wake up in the morning with Jesus thoughts and honor ringing its bell loudly in our hearts and minds. Then at some point during that same day, here comes our little fleshly nature rearing its ugly head. And when this happens, what must immediately take place is the replacing of that dishonorable thought with an honorable one. We must let Paul's words resonate with us in a way that allows us to not only cast that dishonorable thought down but also to see God's goodness in things that are honorable.

Because we live in a corrupt world and have a corrupt nature, it would be easy to overlook all of God's goodness. And you're probably wondering, *How did we go from honor to God's goodness?* Well, it's simple. Apart from God's goodness it's impossible to recognize things that are worthy of honor and respect. When God created the heavens and the earth, His daily affirmation stood in the words "and God saw that it was good." What God looked upon was to be adored, praised, and seen as something beautiful, therefore honorable. This is confirmed by how we see later in the first chapter of Genesis the attitude of God toward all creation: "And God saw everything that He had made, and behold, it was very good." If in all of God's creation, He saw goodness and we are now living in God's creation, we should recognize His goodness, too. And this should cause us to esteem God's things as things that deserve respect and honor. Anything else that is not of God can't possibly invoke that feeling in us because anything opposite of good is not of God and would not be honorable.

When we think about our lives as Christians, all that we do should point back to Christ, and those observing should grow to value Him in the same way we do. We are to show respect to all the venerable objects of society, when they are not in violation of the Law of God. We are to honor one another, and, most importantly, we are to honor God. And by thinking on honorable things, this will always be the product of our words and actions. Honor will be the constant posture of our hearts because it will be the constant state of our minds.

DOING THE
WORK: HONORABLE

PRAYER

Dear Lord,

Thank You for Your beautiful creation and for allowing me to be able to see Your honor in it all. I ask that You guide me as I go through life seeking You and working to live honorably. Help me to address anything in my life that is not honorable so that I can give it to You for You to purge from my life. As I grow closer to You, help others to see the honor in me that flows from Your grace. And bless them to desire the same for their lives.

THINGS TO CONSIDER:

1. Do I struggle with thinking and acting honorably daily?
2. Do I allow my dishonorable thoughts to affect my actions each day?
3. Are there things that I need to address in my life that would help me to think and act more honorably?

SCRIPTURES TO READ:

- Isaiah 26:3
- Romans 12:17
- Philippians 4:8
- James 1:17

My Notes

My Notes

Section

Three

Staying Focused

$\mathcal{T}he \mathcal{T}orn$ **MILLENNIAL: PART 1**

DEVOTION

> Lord, I'm split in two. Part of me loves the world
> and the other loves You.

These words to a well-known gospel song by artist Jonathan McReynolds echo the sentiments of so many believers. But just because so many believers feel this way, is it meant to be this way? And if it is this way, can it stay this way?

It's nearly impossible to go through life without preferences. We either want vanilla or chocolate, blue or black, sweet or unsweet, and the list goes on. We just like things a certain way and whether by nature or nurture, we've learned to not compromise too much on these particulars. Although I don't always like to admit it, I am a somewhat … well, maybe, very … particular person. And one thing I am unwaveringly particular about is how I like my coffee.

I am not among the elitists who prefer an Iced Caramel Macchiato or a Cappuccino on Ice in the morning. I am your basic, hot coffee drinker who will sometimes spruce things up with a Vanilla or seasonal Chestnut Praline Latte from Starbucks. But they must be hot. The thought of lukewarm coffee unsettles my stomach and reminds me of what Jesus says in Revelation when He addresses the church in Laodicea: "I know your works: you are neither cold nor hot. Would that you were either cold or hot! So, because you are lukewarm, and neither hot nor cold, I will spit you out of My mouth" (Revelation 3:15–16). And this is exactly what I want to do when I sip my once piping hot coffee to discover that it is lukewarm.

When we think about our own preferences and how we respond when there are deviations from these preferences, it should prompt us to think about how God feels when we deviate from the standard that He's set for our lives. I remember when I initially heard this Jonathan McReynolds song, "No Gray," I was at this very stage in my life—wanting a surplus of the world but wanting a dab of Christ, too. My attraction to the world worked assiduously to dilute my desire to please God. The world and all its fleeting wonders appealed to me in a way that only God did when the world let me down. As so many of us "ex-fence-herders" are aware of, each time I was torn between the two, I knew this was not God's way.

As believers, we are called to be different from those who are of the world. I'll bring to your remembrance Jesus saying that those who belong to Him are "not of the world" (John 17:14–16) and James urging believers to "keep themselves unstained from the world" (James 1:27). So, in a world where culture is becoming increasingly popular and influencers are pervading our homes with all their knowledge and expertise, how do we live out this instruction? How do we stay accurately informed, contextually sound, and effective while remaining adherent to God's Word? How do we know if we are conforming or being transformed if so many believers and unbelievers look the same? How do we go from being torn to being sure?

"It'd be cool if we could love the Lord and still go do our thing. But see, it doesn't work like that. You gotta be white or black." (Jonathan McReynolds, "No Gray")

DOING THE
WORK: TORN 1

PRAYER

Dear Lord,

As I seek to navigate living in this world while not becoming a partaker of the sin of this world, help me to see Your goodness and Your grace. Open my eyes so that I can see Your heart when I choose to straddle the fence of the world and Your Word. I want to choose You daily while still being able to effectively bring others to the light of Your glory. Help me to do this with peace, joy, and an understanding of how much better my life will be by surrendering it to You.

THINGS TO CONSIDER:

1. Is there anything in culture that is influencing me more than Christ?
2. Am I currently experiencing wanting more of the world than I do of the Lord?
3. Would I consider myself a lukewarm Christian? And if so, in what ways?

SCRIPTURES TO READ:

- John 17
- James 1:27
- Revelation 3:15–16

My Notes

My Notes

$\mathcal{T}he \; \mathcal{T}orn$ MILLENNIAL: PART 2

Week 10

DEVOTION

> I'd rather stand with God and be judged by the
> world than stand with the world and be judged
> by God.
>
> —*God's Not Dead 2*

Last week, we were left with unanswered questions to think about. So, this week, we'll seek to answer those questions.

In an age where the popularity and influence of social media is at an all-time high, it's easy to get lured into the "trend" vortex. From what to wear to who you can marry to burning sage, we are met with so many varying perspectives on what we should or should not do. And while everyone who's anyone with a computer and phone can be an expert, the information offered bears little validity without the undergirding of scripture. A part of why culture and the world have become so increasingly attractive, I believe, has a lot to do with visibility. Because we are now able to see other people live their lives publicly, we are drawn in and tempted to mimic what we observe (and let's be honest, for a split second, the result of our observation appeals to us as enjoyable and the attention gratifying). But what we should consider is maybe, just maybe, our lack of discipline to deprive ourselves of the need to "scroll" is simply due to our lack of a *stronger* affinity to God's Word. Because through it and it alone will we be able to resist the desire to conform to what we see.

Let's take a stroll down memory lane to the Garden of Eden. When Satan came to deceive Eve, he was able to lure her by manipulating the function of what she saw. This is what we read in Genesis 3:6: "So when the woman *saw* that the tree was good for food, and that it was a delight *to the eyes*, and that the tree was to be desired to make one wise, she took of its fruit and ate, and she also gave some to her husband who was with her, and he ate." And just as Eve was deceived in the garden, so are we deceived today. By the same method via the same sense: sight. Therefore, to live out James's instruction to remain unstained from the world, we must recognize whether what we see is a product of the world or a tool given by God to be used in the world. And then we must believe and trust what God's Word says about Himself, about us, and about what He will do for us if we obey Him. This is how we can trust that the tree of life is the one and only tree that we need.

The world has implemented certain systems that endeavor to satisfy everyone. Believers are almost made to be tolerant and compliant with worldly standards whether through legislation, media, fashion, or medicine. But what all believers must understand is that God, the Creator, has already set the standard. When we conform to anything other than this, we are indirectly (or maybe directly) telling God that what He established for us is not right, not worth trusting, not what's best for our lives, and that He isn't valuable enough for us to sacrifice our desires for His perfect will. Booker T. Washington said, "A lie doesn't become truth, wrong doesn't become right, and evil doesn't become good just because it's accepted by a majority." And this couldn't be more true as we see more and more believers being persuaded by those in the world. Paul brings to our attention, in his second letter to Timothy, that Demas, a fellow worker in the gospel, left him because he "loved this present world" (2 Timothy 4:10). And just as this was a challenge in the early church, it still is today. But something that we neglect to consider is that because of who the prince of this world is, all the world is good for is to steal, kill, and destroy. And every effort on our part to seek satisfaction from the world will drive us deeper into dissatisfaction because of the nature of the destructive results the world produces in our lives.

Satan's ultimate goal is to strip us of our faith so that we doubt God, His goodness, and the reality of the manifestation of

His promises to us. But this is why it is imperative to know how we should live as believers. Believers produce the fruit of the Spirit—love, joy, peace, patience, kindness, goodness, faithfulness, gentleness, and self-control—because we have crucified the flesh with its passion and desires (Galatians 5:22–24). In knowing this, it becomes evident that those who do not exhibit these characteristics are those who are known as "workers of the flesh." And this distinguishes those on the believing team from those who are allowing Satan to steal, kill, and destroy their lives.

If you take a peek at the works of the flesh mentioned in Galatians 5—sexual immorality, impurity, idolatry, jealousy, fits of anger, and the list goes on to name twelve more—you'll notice that these are all things that lead to chaos, hurt, pain, division, and devastation. Hence, "works" of the flesh versus "fruit" of the Spirit. What we do as a result of our fleshly desires being carried out is defined as "works" possibly because they are divided and often cause a betrayal, even of the flesh itself. But the fruit produced from the Spirit is singular because no matter how numerous the results, they still form a unified and harmonious whole. So, when in search of evidence that points to whether you or someone else is conforming or being transformed, look no further than works or fruit.

In a world that has believers so torn and often confronted with so many options that seem right, we must stand firm on the promises of God and believe that He knows and possesses what's best for our lives. But as we stand on this, we also can't isolate and detach ourselves from what's going on around us so that we render ourselves ineffective and unsuccessful in the war against the attacks of the enemy. Just like we're in our own spiritual fight as a believer, so are other believers. And unbeknownst to unbelievers in the world, they are as well. Because of this, believers need each other to stay informed of what's happening around us to continue to provide encouragement and support to one another and do as Galatians 6:2 says and "bear one another's burdens." And those who are of the world need our witness. They need our testimony that confirms the power of God in our lives.

And we provide this witness and testimony in a way that resonates with where they are but upholds the message of the gospel of Jesus Christ. But first, we must make a choice—a choice between "the ones who can kill our body or the One who can condemn our body and soul" (Matthew 10:28). When we make the choice to choose Christ, He will guide us as we navigate this cruel world. This choice is how we stay accurately informed, contextually sound, and effective in our ministry. This is how we confirm the stance we should take as believers in a world that wants to strip us of our identity in Christ. And this is how we allow God's love to drive us closer to Him so that we can work to change culture instead of conforming and allowing culture to change us.

DOING THE WORK: TORN 2

PRAYER

Dear Lord,

As I continue to seek to navigate living in this world while not becoming a partaker of the sin of this world, help me to always see Your goodness and Your grace. I want to know and fully trust what Your Word says, and I want to live this out in a way that produces the fruit of Your Spirit. Help me to not fall victim to the world and its lure but to convince the world of who You are and how Your ways are higher and better. Father, keep me as I strive each day to do as Christ did and please You.

THINGS TO CONSIDER:

1. What do my actions each day say about my choice to choose Christ or the world?
2. Am I producing the fruit of the Spirit or carrying out the works of the flesh in my life?
3. Am I making steps toward no longer being a lukewarm Christian and fully surrendering my life to the Lord?

SCRIPTURES TO READ:

- Proverbs 14:12
- Proverbs 30:12
- Romans 10:3
- Galatians 5
- Galatians 6:2

My Notes

My Notes

The Tempted MILLENNIAL: PART 1

DEVOTION

> Go into all the world and proclaim the Gospel to
> the whole creation.
>
> —Mark 16:15 ESV

Before we jump right into temptation, let's talk about the gospel. In Luke 4:18, Jesus said that the Spirit of the Lord appointed Him to proclaim good news (the gospel) to the poor. So, when Jesus said this, what exactly does He mean? What was so good about what Jesus was proclaiming?

Usually good news is considered "good news" because of the results the news renders. In the case of the gospel, Jesus was carrying the message that there was someone who had come to give up Himself and His life to take on the sins of the world so that the world can be saved. That means for those who will accept this teaching, they are no longer responsible for carrying their own sins. They are no longer obligated to sacrifice animals or go to the high priest to be pardoned. They now have someone who will bear the wrath of God on Himself at the cross. Someone to take on the guilt of the world so that all can be reconciled to God and deemed not guilty even though they really are. If you haven't heard any good news lately, today is your day because that right there is *good news*!

In this verse, notice that Jesus said He was preaching the gospel to the poor. Jesus was coming to proclaim the good news to those who were poor in spirit and who were void of something. The reason the gospel is preached to and accepted by the poor is because they are in search of something that they are lacking and that they acknowledge they can't provide themselves. The gospel gives the poor Christ and His delivering power. This is how the poor differ from the rich and why it's harder to reach the rich and for them to enter the kingdom, as Jesus said. The rich have formed a sense of dependence on themselves. They reject the idea that they need someone outside of themselves for anything, when who they really need to depend on is Christ more than anyone else. All of us can gain so much more in Christ than we can from ourselves or anyone else.

In accepting Christ, we embrace His delivering power. This means that we are rescued, carried away to safety, snatched from danger, and we escape something. But what are we delivered from when we accept Christ into our lives? Romans 8:2 says that we are "free from the law of sin and death." Death would have been our judgment and will be for those who won't accept Christ. And this is not just a physical death but a spiritual death where one will be separated from God forever. Hence, if we die in Christ, we are at rest, but a death outside of Christ is eternal torment. Sin leads to death, but we are delivered from the bondage of sin and death if we accept Christ's redemptive work on the cross. This causes us to be delivered from continually committing sinful acts here on Earth that can and will lead to eternal torment.

But what's so awesome about this is that in deliverance we aren't just saved or rescued or snatched away from sin and death and judgment. We're also given something. We aren't just taken from a bad situation to be left on our own to fend for ourselves. We are taken from a bad situation and put in an even better one. And we are given the Holy Spirit to help us live out our faith in response to our deliverance. And this is where temptation slowly creeps into the conversation.

I think it's fair to ask this question: Will we be tempted as believers to do wrong or sin once we are delivered from sin and death? A lot of people may think one of two ways. They either think that once you're saved, you no longer must fight off temptation and that it's always going to be smooth sailing. Or they think that once you accept Christ as Savior, you can do whatever you want because you've eternally been granted absolution. Sadly, neither of the two are true.

Jesus said in John 16:33: "I have said these things to you, that in Me you may have peace. In the world you will have tribulation. But take heart; I have overcome the world." So, this dispels the idea that we won't go through, but in Christ, no matter what we go through (which most of the time, for the believer, it will be for the sake of Christ) we always have peace in Christ because we know He has already defeated the outcome of what the world tries to bring our way. Paul says in Romans 6:1–2: "shall we continue in sin that grace may abound? God forbid! How shall we that are dead to sin still live in it?" This rids us of the idea that we can live how we want and still profess a life of deliverance. And 1 John 3:4, 10 tells us that anyone who practices sin practices lawlessness and that anyone who makes a practice of sin is a child of the devil.

We will be tempted as believers—inwardly and outwardly—because of the flesh, or the sin nature that remains in us, and because of what Satan will try to use to take us off course. But if, with our hearts and minds, we serve and give ourselves over to the law of God, we won't yield to our flesh and become captive to the law of sin.

As we walk in our deliverance, is it safe to trust that we have the power, on our own, to overcome sin and temptation? I wish that were true, but it is not. But the Holy Spirit in us does possess this power because He can't do wrong. This power that resides in us is who we must yield to so that He can lead us and not our flesh, and this is simply because He can't sin, and we can.

At one time, I was of the persuasion that because I knew right from wrong, I could control what I did or didn't do with sheer will power. But as life started coming at me, and I started giving in to things that I didn't think I would ever do, my mind-set slowly but surely shifted. It wasn't until I stopped relying on myself and realized how fragile I was that I started to allow the Holy Spirit to walk me through life in this world. This is the only empowerment any of us have to resist carrying out the desires of our flesh.

I know this is hard to accept because we feel as though our flesh is who we are and who we can stay committed to. But our flesh is really sick. God, however, is really good in that He gave us Someone to help overcome it. And because of this precious gift, we must understand that there is not a struggle in the world or anything we can face that the Holy Spirit hasn't already defeated and overcome. This means that because He lives in us, we can overcome, too.

DOING THE
WORK: TEMPTED 1

PRAYER

Dear Lord,

Thank You for giving the world the Way to be reconciled to You. Thank You for sending Your Son, Jesus Christ, to die on Calvary to save the world from their sins. I thank You that I am amongst the family of those who can partake in the fullness of salvation and deliverance. And I thank You that Your wrath has been satisfied for my life through my Savior, Jesus Christ. Continue to lead and direct my life so that I can do as Jesus did and proclaim the good news to others with joy, gladness, and boldness.

THINGS TO CONSIDER:

1. Does my life show thankfulness for the sacrifice of Christ?
2. Are there areas in my life that I need to give over to the Lord to be delivered from?
3. Am I aware that how I view the gospel and my deliverance can determine how I deal with temptation?

SCRIPTURES TO READ:

- Luke 4:16–19
- Romans 6:1–2
- Romans 8:1–2
- 1 John 3:1–10

My Notes

My Notes

The Tempted **MILLENNIAL: PART 2**

DEVOTION

> But each person is tempted when he is lured and
> enticed by his own desire.
>
> —James 1:14 ESV

If you're anything like me, you love a good example! One that invokes a feeling within you that places you right there on the scene amid all the action. Good thing for us as believers, as we deal with temptation, we have the perfect example of overcoming it. Matthew 4 gives us a front-row seat to the temptation of Christ by Satan. This encounter recorded in the Gospels shows us the three ways Jesus was tempted, which sheds light on how we will be tempted also: lust of the flesh, lust of the eyes, and pride of life.

Let's be clear, Jesus wasn't born with a sin nature. Even though He was born of a woman (to be our kinsman-redeemer), and He took on our sins and the penalty and power that sin had over us, He Himself was still sinless by divine nature and as a human being. This means that He wasn't battling anything internally that would cause Him to yield to temptation. So, what does this tell us? If Jesus is in us through the Person of the Holy Spirit, then we cannot say that the Spirit in us ever tempts us with anything. The Bible says no man can say when he is tempted that he is tempted of God (James 1:13), and this is true for any and every believer. And this also tells us something else that we'll discover here momentarily.

It's amazing how much credit we give Satan even in the absence of the possession of all power. Satan is so blinded by pride and greed that he is incapable of conceding to the Person of Christ. His own wickedness obscured his ability to recognize who he was dealing with, which should've made him rethink tempting Christ all together. But pride always gets the best of him, just like it did as Lucifer in heaven and still does as Satan on earth. Pride also causes us to make some very unwise decisions that, to us, seem purposeful, but what scripture says is true, "pride goeth before destruction," because that's ultimately what happens.

Because Satan is so bothered by God, he allowed himself to be fooled into thinking that he could tempt God Himself (because Christ is 100 percent God and was 100 percent man) all because of what he thought he saw in the *man* of Christ. And this is exactly how he feels about us hoping it results in us forsaking God. But the presence of the Holy Spirit brings out an immutable fact about the believer: Satan is not smarter or wiser than us. But he is tricky because we don't operate in that space of deceit. In knowing this, we should always be prepared for when he comes to attack us.

When we look at this temptation encounter in Matthew, we see that Satan tempted Jesus with things he felt would appeal to Him. How naive, right?!

- Christ had recently fasted forty days, so He was hungry. Satan offered bread.
- Satan took Jesus up to the pinnacle of the temple and told Christ to make an attempt on His own life because the angels would save Him.
- Satan took Christ to a high mountain and offered Him all the kingdoms of the world and their glory if He worshipped him.

Although Christ was 100 percent man and is 100 percent God, the divine nature of Christ will overrule the man of Christ every time. Remember when I said that "this also tells us something else that we'll discover here momentarily?" Well, here we are. As 100 percent human beings, we should be able to withstand temptation because we should unceasingly be conceding to the

Holy Spirit, or the 100 percent God inside of us, just as Christ did. Though our flesh is sick and powerful, it is not more powerful than God, and if we relinquish the control that it has by giving that control over to God, we will be able to imitate Christ in all things, even resisting temptation.

If you're curious like me, you may have wondered why, since Christ couldn't be tempted, He was led away to be tempted in the first place? The language in this passage suggests that this interaction was meant to happen: "Jesus was *led* up by the Spirit into the wilderness *to be tempted* [emphasis added]" (Matthew 4:1). In this encounter, we see that this was a visible manifestation of a spiritual matter. Compare this to how we are attacked now. We don't see Satan, our sin nature, and we don't physically see God, but here in scripture, these two were encountering one another in a face-to-face interaction.

We can get the inside track on how this visibly took place, but now this happens spiritually for us. This encounter shows us how temptation and Satan will come at us to tempt us, but Christ shows us physically and spiritually how to overcome. Christ used the Word of God to ward off Satan. Christ spoke (physical) by saying what the Word said, and He allowed His divine nature (spiritual) to fight against what His flesh felt—He was hungry, but He didn't yield.

We must remember that God is sinless in His nature. Therefore, there is nothing that can cause Him to sin, not even temptation from *outside* of Him, because nothing *in* Him will yield to it. This is our fail-proof example of how we should allow the Holy Spirit to overrule our flesh or the human part of us that is capable of sinning. And this is also an example of how using the Word of God wards off the enemy. The Spirit in us resists, and the Word of God makes the enemy flee.

As believers, we have God in us by way of the Holy Spirit, which is who we submit to. And although there is a battle between our flesh, Satan, and God, Jesus resisting the temptation of Satan shows us that the power of the One we have pledged allegiance to leaves us void of any excuse to sin or yield to any form of temptation. So, by yielding to the same power that enabled Jesus to resist, we see exactly how we can resist all the same.

DOING THE WORK: TEMPTED 2

PRAYER

Dear Lord,

As I face the world, Satan, and my flesh each day, help me to utilize Your Word and Your power to not yield to temptation. I acknowledge that the attacks of the enemy and my flesh are real and that it takes Your Holy Spirit within me to war against them. I want to continually activate Your power so that I can effectively ward off any attempt to take me from You. Because I have You, I know that I can overcome all things and that in You, all evil that will come against me is already defeated.

THINGS TO CONSIDER:

1. How often do I fall victim to yielding to temptation?
2. Is there anything in my life that I am struggling with that is causing me to constantly be tempted?
3. How does my acknowledgment of the power of the Holy Spirit help me properly view temptation?

SCRIPTURES TO READ:

- Matthew 4:1–11
- 1 Corinthians 10:13
- James 1:13–15

My Notes

My Notes

$\mathcal{T}he\ \mathcal{S}exually$ TEMPTED MILLENNIAL

Week 13

DEVOTION

> Or do you not know that your body is a temple of
> the Holy Spirit within you, whom you have from
> God? You are not your own, for you were bought
> with a price. So glorify God in your body.
> —1 Corinthians 6:19–20 ESV

An idea that has been widely accepted today is that sex sells.
Some millennials, Gen Z individuals, and even some Baby
Boomers seem to be complacent with the idea that their body
counts don't matter and that it's a major accomplishment to
not be a virgin before marriage. Promiscuity is promoted. It is
bragged about in songs, movies, and on television series. We
see sex everywhere. And not that I am exempt. I have had my
dealings with the premarital sex sin myself. But thank God, I have
been delivered and am continuing to rely on the Holy Spirit to
keep me. What I realize is that having to commit to not engaging
on my own without the help of someone more powerful than my
fleshly desires is impossible.

So, in a society that oversells sex and pushes the consumption
of sexual content, how do we promote abstinence and celibacy
without seeming stringent, rigid, legalistic, and hypercritical?
How do we compete with the overarching message that sex
outside of marriage is acceptable? How do we ask people to give
up something they *like* for someone greater to *love*? How do we
perpetuate the message that being a virgin is still attractive or
that abstinence is favorable? How do we convey the message
that sex outside of marriage is not God's plan or design?

How about we start at the beginning? When we look at Genesis, we see the exact origin of sex. God gave Adam and Eve the command to be fruitful and multiply and replenish the earth. He gave them a command to do what was appropriate and convenient for the increase of humankind and for the filling of the earth with inhabitants, which we see in Isaiah 45:18. This shows that marriage is an ordinance of God that was instituted in the Garden and that procreation is natural and may be performed without sin.

We see, on numerous occasions in scripture, how and where sex is to be practiced. In Corinthians, Galatians, and Thessalonians, fornication, or premarital sex, is not condoned by God and for good cause. An increasing worldview today tells people that being a Christian is being a part of a very tyrannical, anarchical type of faith. However, it's not a democracy because we've already been given the guide for holy living. But if you think about what it saves you from, then you'll see why the Bible tells you to stay away from certain things.

Frivolous, incautious sex can come with unwanted results—pregnancy, diseases, soul ties, stalkers, heartbreak, and a lot of other implications that we don't necessarily desire, if we're honest. And that goes for so many other sins or things that keep us from living peaceful, joyful, holy lives. This is why it's important to appreciate what someone who loves you will warn you against to potentially save your life.

I'm not sure how familiar you are with the paradox of hedonism, but it points out that the more we seek out pleasure, the less we enjoy it because it may not yield the results we seek. Our lack of discipline and self-control is what can put us in situations that fuel the wrong sexual desires. One wrong decision, one wrong person, one too many lustful conversations can have us living with lingering consequences that resulted from only a moment of pseudosatisfaction that's void of true fulfillment.

The Bible urges us to "flee from sexual immorality," because "every other sin a person commits is outside the body, but the sexually immoral person sins against his own body" (1 Corinthians 6:18). Our bodies are temples of the Holy Spirit within us, so they don't belong to us, and if we want to protect, preserve, respect, and honor these temples, we must watch what we do with our temple and with whom we do it.

In knowing the consequences of unwise sexual decisions and defining where sex should exist and how sex within this existence pleases God, it can be concluded that sex is only as good as the God who created it. And because we know God to be greater than anything that exists (because He is God, and He is the Creator), He must be better than sex. Thinking on a spiritual level tells us that if the God who created sex is better than sex and sex is designed for marriage, if we are unmarried and engage in sex outside of marriage, we are fundamentally saying to God, "the sex You created for me to enjoy in marriage is better than You?"

Holy living should be an action governed by the goal to gain eternal life (Romans 8:18; John 3:16; Philippians 1:21). Just think, everything we experience here that we enjoy, the right way, won't come close to what we will experience with God. And although when we mention sex, it automatically connotes negativity, sex, when done right, is an act of joining together in oneness with the person God gave you. In acknowledging this, don't you just think that since God gave sex in marriage, that the sex inside that God-ordained, God-designed marriage will be better than all those meaningless connections that you may or may not remember?

Our flesh is a sick thing, and it always leaves us searching for more. Sin leaves us searching for more because it's not fulfilling. By saving ourselves for the spouse God has ordained for us, we can save ourselves from committing an act of sin, from feelings of shame, disappointment, and regret, and from feeling misused. We can also save ourselves from the unknown. Let's face it, unless the Holy Spirit reveals someone to us, we don't really know a person, and by giving our bodies to someone that we don't truly know, we take a chance with our health and our heart, neither of which should be taken lightly.

Remember, the desires of the flesh are against the Spirit (Galatians 5:17), so we must discipline ourselves, through the Word, to garner the strength to say no to deviant sexual desires. And we also must realize that a good way to overcome the desire to partake in sinful sexual acts is to not intentionally open avenues for that desire to overtake us.

If this were easy, everyone would get it right, but the truth is that it's not. And since God knows just how powerful our flesh is, He gave us His Word and Himself, who is all powerful. We just have to let this power work within us (Ephesians 3:20) so that we will be spiritually prepared at all times for attacks that may come our way, even if those attacks come from our own flesh. I know a lot of people who wish they would've done things differently, me being one of them. But I also know a lot of people who are thankful that God spared them throughout the years of their careless and negligent behavior. No matter what culture says, there is nothing wrong with saving yourself for marriage, and if you haven't, there is still time to start over. Don't fall victim to your flesh; plenty of us already have. And if you were to poll others who had it to do all over again, I'm sure they would tell you that by only giving your body to the one God has prepared for you, you are saving yourself to save yourself.

DOING THE WORK:
SEXUALLY TEMPTED

PRAYER

Dear Lord,

As I navigate a life that is given in service to You, help me to give my sexual desires to You to change into a burning desire to please You. Whether I'm married or single, help me to surrender any desire that is not of You to Your healing power. And if I am not struggling with sexual desires myself, give me the courage to witness to others about Your plan for their lives as it deals with sex. I want to commit my body to You and You alone, and I want others to see the benefit of this, too.

THINGS TO CONSIDER:

1. Am I currently struggling with sexual desires that are contrary to God's Word?
2. If I have been delivered, how can I use my experience with a sinful sexual past to help others?
3. Does society in any way play a role in how I view premarital sex?

SCRIPTURES TO READ:

- Genesis 1:27–28
- 1 Corinthians 7:2
- 1 Thessalonians 4:3–4

My Notes

My Notes

Epilogue
STRENGTH FOR THE JOURNEY

Hi there! You made it through volume 1 of this devotional, and I couldn't be more excited for you! I hope that each devotional opened your eyes to some truth about yourself, God, and how living each day to the glory of God not only benefits the kingdom but also benefits you. My heart's desire is that all of us can become an expression of God's heart here on earth—a mighty army full of true, devoted, bold ambassadors for Jesus Christ!

When you close this book, tuck it away, and move on with your life, my prayer is that you let these words settle into your heart and lead you to God's Word with a zeal like never before. The Lord honors it, fellow saints rejoice in it, and the world needs it. I don't want my name, this book, or the stories to be what stay with you; I want the gospel of Jesus Christ to remain *in* you and His name reverberating in the world *because of* you.

All in all, when you close this book, I only ask this of you.

Let your mind be daily transformed,
Let true worship be given,
Let your light shine,
And let God's glory be revealed in it all.

Five Tips for Studying God's Word

1. Ask the Holy Spirit for understanding of the scriptures.
   - Who better to reveal to you what you need to know than the Person who inspired every word?

2. Eliminate preconceived bias, determinations, and interpretations.
   - Don't become so focused on how you want to apply a passage that you miss the overall message of the passage.

3. Ask yourself this important question.
   - How does this passage I am reading unite with the overall theme of the Bible?

4. Be cognizant of *how* you interpret what you read.
   - Don't seek to apply a passage from where you want to go. See it based on where it needs to take you.

5. Always keep scripture in context.
   - To do this, you need to gather all historical, cultural, literary, and linguistic information surrounding the text.

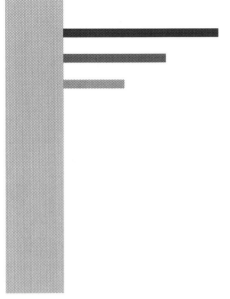

ABOUT THE AUTHOR

Brittany Dodson,
PharmD, MABS

Brittany is a Christian artist, writer, evangelist, pharmacist, and podcast host. She received her Associate of Arts from the University of Central Arkansas, a Master of Arts in Biblical Studies from Moody Bible Institute, and a Doctor of Pharmacy from the University of Arkansas for Medical Sciences.

She currently serves as youth director, assistant choir director, and coordinates Women's Ministry activities at the Freedom Missionary Baptist Church, where she is an active member. Driven to use her speaking and teaching gifts to share the gospel of Jesus Christ, she started *The Traditional Millennial Podcast*—a podcast created by a millennial for millennials who still embrace tradition.

Brittany loves her family, traveling, keeping up with fashion, and has a passion and appreciation for teaching the Word of God.

Printed in the United States
by Baker & Taylor Publisher Services